Avalanches

AVALANCHE AREA
NEXT 1 MILE

DO NOT STOP

Anastasia Suen

Rourke
Educational Media

rourkeeducationalmedia.com

Before Reading:

Building Academic Vocabulary and Background Knowledge

Before reading a book, it is important to tap into what your child or students already know about the topic. This will help them develop their vocabulary, increase their reading comprehension, and make connections across the curriculum.

1. *Look at the cover of the book. What will this book be about?*
2. *What do you already know about the topic?*
3. *Let's study the Table of Contents. What will you learn about in the book's chapters?*
4. *What would you like to learn about this topic? Do you think you might learn about it from this book? Why or why not?*
5. *Use a reading journal to write about your knowledge of this topic. Record what you already know about the topic and what you hope to learn about the topic.*
6. *Read the book.*
7. *In your reading journal, record what you learned about the topic and your response to the book.*
8. *After reading the book complete the activities below.*

Content Area Vocabulary
Read the list. What do these words mean?

avalanche
cornice
crown
crust
debris
flanks
fracture
powder
probe
runout zone
snowpack
stauchwall

After Reading:

Comprehension and Extension Activity

After reading the book, work on the following questions with your child or students in order to check their level of reading comprehension and content mastery.

1. *What is the difference between hard and soft slabs of snow? (Summarize)*
2. *Explain why high elevation makes for colder temperatures? (Infer)*
3. *Why is it important to create a snow pit and check the snow? (Asking questions)*
4. *How do you survive an avalanche? (Text to self connection)*
5. *How can avalanches change ecosystems? (Asking questions)*

Extension Activity

Pretend you work for a ski resort. Part of your job is to inform guests about avalanche safety. Create a brochure, poster, or presentation that explains how avalanches form and how to stay safe during one. Share your creation with classmates, teachers, or parents. Afterward, see what they remember by asking them questions!

Table of Contents

Avalanche!

The snow on the mountainside is on the move. No, it's not just snowflakes falling down from the clouds. This is more than mere precipitation. A giant slab of fallen snow has broken loose and it is coming down the mountain fast. It's an **avalanche**!

As the avalanche of snow comes rapidly down the steep mountainside, it covers everything in its way. It covers skiers and snowboarders. It covers snowmobiles and mountain cabins. Nothing can stop it.

Ninety percent of avalanche victims die in slides triggered by themselves or a member of their group.

LOVELAND PASS
ELEVATION 11,990 FT.

CONTINENTAL DIVIDE

DEPARTMENT OF AGRICULTURE

Snowboarding Disaster

On a Saturday afternoon in April 2013, six snowboarders went up the mountain to Loveland Pass in Colorado. But only one came home alive. The six were snowboarding at nearly 11,990 feet (3,655 meters) when they triggered an avalanche. The slide, almost 600 feet (183 meters) wide and 8 feet (2.43 meters) deep, buried the entire party. One snowboarder dug himself out of the snow and called for help.

Located in the Rocky Mountains of north-central Colorado, Loveland Pass is a high mountain pass that is both beautiful and deadly.

Snow in the mountains is a way of life. At some elevations, there is snow on the peaks year-round. Farther down the mountainside, the snow is more than just beauty to appreciate. As the snow melts, it flows into the aquifers that we use for our water supply.

So how do mountain dwellers cope with avalanches? They look for the signs. If you know what to look for, you can actually predict an avalanche.

Did You Know?
Avalanches can change the ecosystem. Avalanches break trees in half or pull them out of the ground. This makes room for new trees to grow. An old forest will have new growth.

Before skiing, hiking, or snowmobiling in the backcountry, an area not maintained by a ski resort or the National Park Service, taking an avalanche safety course is a good idea.

Members of the American Avalanche Association teach classes. They are for people who want to go out into the backcountry. Before they go out in the snow, they need to know about avalanches. They need to look for these six red flags.

Red Flag No. 1: Recent Avalanches

If there are new avalanches in the area that means more avalanches could happen. The conditions that cause the snow to break apart and slide downhill don't just occur in one location. If one part of the mountainside is coming down, chances are another section may slide downhill, too.

When snow splits apart, it can make a loud, cracking sound.

Red Flag No. 2: Unstable Snow

As you travel on a mountain, look carefully at the condition of the snow. Nature's warnings are often noisy! If the snow is making extra sounds, that is a sign that the snow is unstable. When snow is unstable it can break easily. If a big chunk breaks, it can start an avalanche.

Whoomph!
When snow collapses, it makes a loud whoomph sound. According to the National Avalanche Center, "whoomph has been adopted as a technical term to describe collapsing snow." If you hear whoomphing, watch out! An avalanche can happen at any time.

Red Flag No. 3: Weak Layers

Unstable snow can be covered up when new snow arrives. The weak layer is buried in the **snowpack**. These weak layers can still cause avalanches. They can happen days or even weeks later. How can you find out where they are? Dig a snow pit to test the snowpack. Check the Avalanche Advisory before traveling out in the snow.

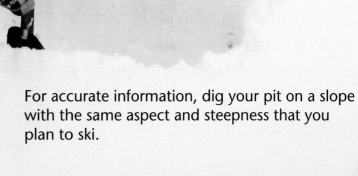

For accurate information, dig your pit on a slope with the same aspect and steepness that you plan to ski.

Watch the Weather

Avalanches often occur on the first day after a storm.

Red Flag No. 4: Recent Rain or Snowfall

Don't be fooled by sunny skies. The mountainside may look beautiful but that doesn't mean that it is safe. The storm has passed, but the damage it did is still there. The rain or snow that fell may have loosened the snowpack, making it unstable. Avalanches often occur on the first day after a storm.

Now or Later?
A direct-action avalanche happens during a storm or just after it ends.

A delayed-action avalanche happens more than 24 hours after a storm.

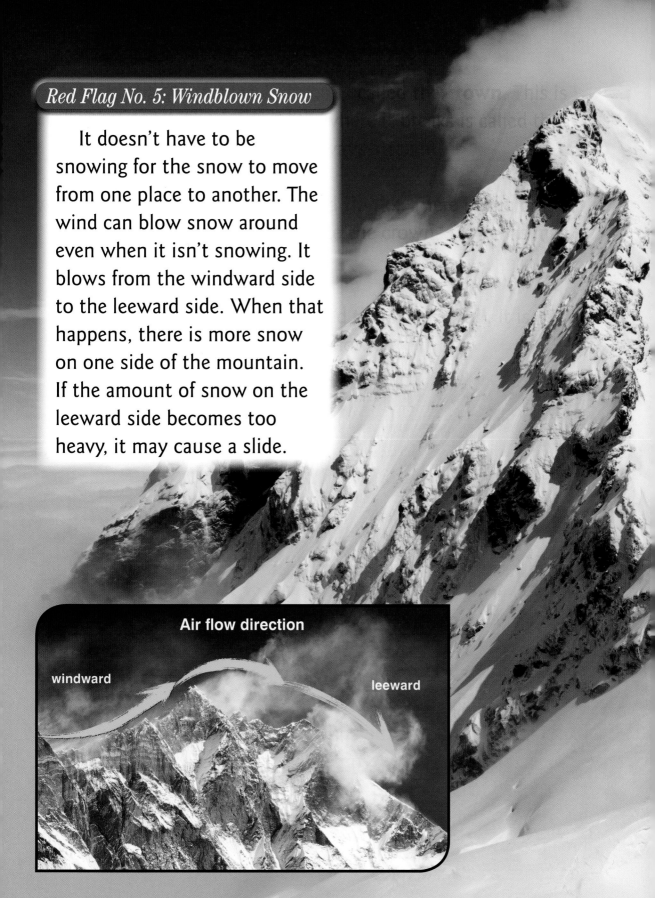

Red Flag No. 5: Windblown Snow

It doesn't have to be snowing for the snow to move from one place to another. The wind can blow snow around even when it isn't snowing. It blows from the windward side to the leeward side. When that happens, there is more snow on one side of the mountain. If the amount of snow on the leeward side becomes too heavy, it may cause a slide.

Air flow direction

windward

leeward

Watery snow can trigger a loose, wet avalanche that falls in a fan pattern.

Red Flag No. 6: Warming Temperatures

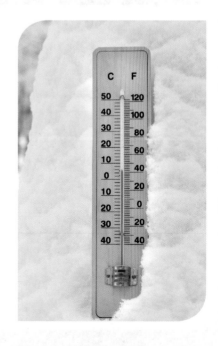

When the temperature rises above the freezing point, the snow begins to melt. That is good news for our water supply. But melting snow can also be bad news. As it melts, the snow begins to move downhill. If the temperature change happens quickly, the snowpack becomes unstable. Unstable snow can break easily. When that happens, it can cause an avalanche.

Will it snow today? What will the temperature be? It is the weather forecaster's job to find out. New snow may trigger an avalanche. Temperature changes can also cause avalanche conditions to develop. Getting the latest news about the weather helps residents to stay prepared. They can watch the weather news on TV or check the weather app on their phone.

Steep Mountains

Avalanches occur in steep, mountainous areas. Wherever there is snow on a steep mountainside there can be an avalanche. Avalanches are most common when the slope is 30 to 45 degrees. What does that look like? A 90 degree angle goes straight up. This is called a right angle. Now draw the third line to make a triangle. This downhill slope is 45 degrees. A 30 degree slope is lower and longer.

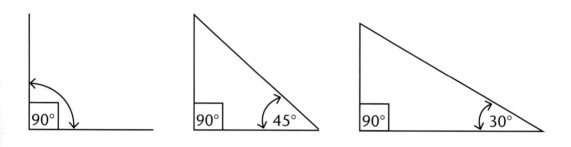

Mount McKinley, in Alaska, is the tallest mountain in North America. Its peak is 20,237 feet (6,168 meters) above sea level.

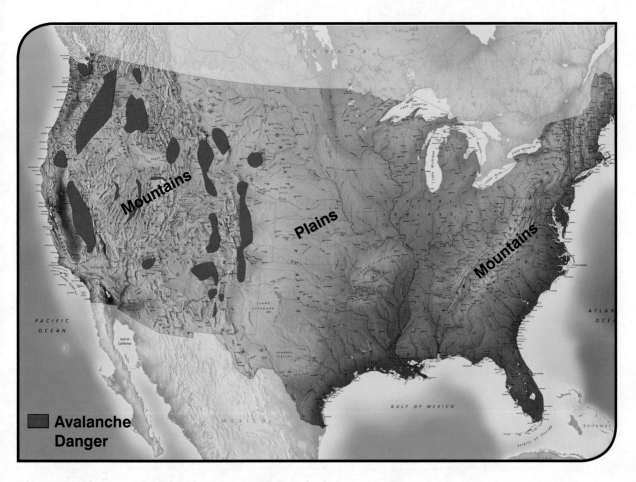

Avalanche Danger

The United States has both mountains and plains.

Did You Know?
Avalanches are possible in the eastern, central, and western parts of the United States.

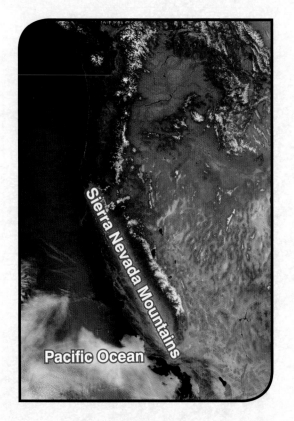

There are mountains all across the United States. Some mountains are near the coast. These are called maritime mountains. The ocean influences the weather here. The wind carries water in from the ocean. It dumps rain and snow on the mountains. Almost all of the water falls on the windward side of these coastal mountains.

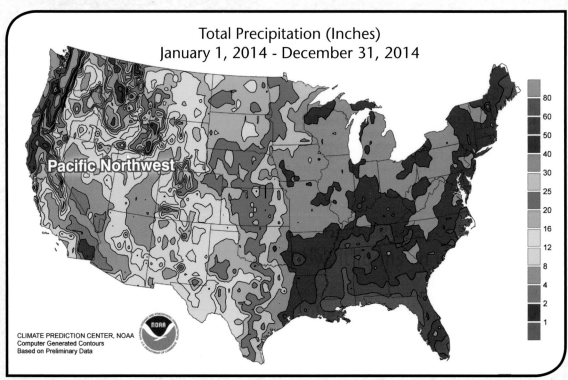

Most of the rain in the Pacific Northwest is near the ocean.

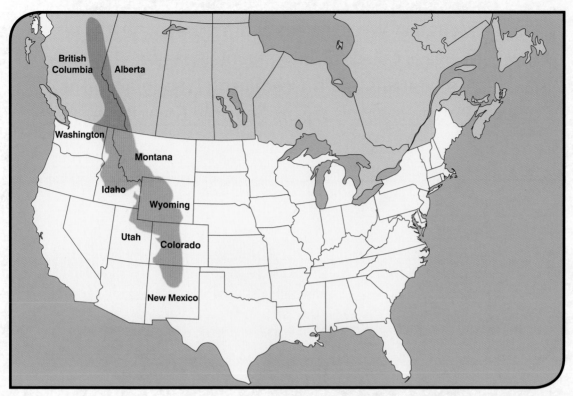

The Rocky Mountains are almost 3,000 miles (4,828 kilometers) long. They stretch across the United States and into Canada.

The Rocky Mountains are a long chain of mountains. There are more than 100 mountain ranges in this mountain chain.

The Rocky Mountains are continental mountains. They are in the middle of the continent. They are also at a high elevation. The high elevation makes the winters very cold. There is a lot of snow, and blizzards are common.

Banff National Park is part of the Canadian Rockies. Moraine Lake is known for its pure, turquoise water.

In the Mountain West there is another area with lots of snow. This area is called the intermountain region. It is between the coastal mountains and the continental mountains. The Colorado Plateau is in this region. So is the Great Basin.

The Intermountain Masters ski races are in Utah, Idaho, and Wyoming.

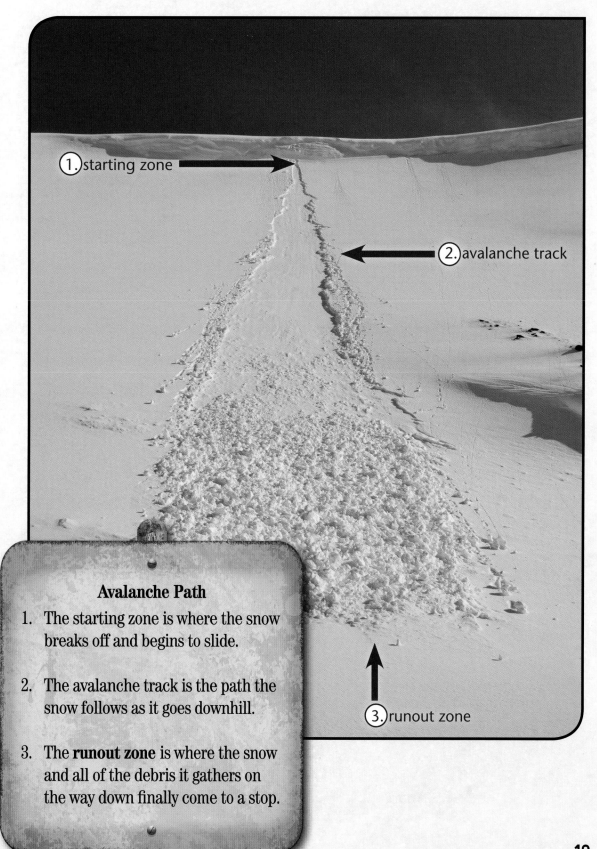

1. starting zone →

2. avalanche track

3. runout zone

Avalanche Path

1. The starting zone is where the snow breaks off and begins to slide.

2. The avalanche track is the path the snow follows as it goes downhill.

3. The **runout zone** is where the snow and all of the debris it gathers on the way down finally come to a stop.

Avalanches can cause delays in transporting goods, services, and emergency vehicles responding to accidents and injuries.

Avalanches don't just slide in the forest. They also cover mountain roads. All traffic stops until the slide can be cleared. No one can get in or out. This makes travel difficult for local residents and for trucks traveling across the region.

To prevent highway closures, road crews practice avalanche control. During off hours, they stop traffic and trigger an avalanche. They use explosives to bring down the unstable snow.

Avalanche Forecasters

Avalanche forecasters work indoors and out. In the field, they dig snow pits and test local conditions. They check the weather stations they have set up in the area. Then they write reports to share with the public. An avalanche forecaster's job is to let people know where avalanches may develop.

Avalanche forecasters study the snowpack to predict avalanches.

Deadly and Destructive Avalanches

A dry snow avalanche occurs in snow below the freezing point. It slides down as a slab or a powder cloud.

Avalanches are deadly and destructive. A **powder** avalanche is very destructive. It starts when a rock or a chunk of ice falls. That fall makes the loose snow slide. The mass of loose snow grows larger and larger as it falls downhill. It can grow both taller and wider as it slides down. Powder avalanches can cover an entire town.

Survivor's Story

Utah Avalanche Center Director Bruce Tremper was caught in a slab avalanche in 1978. It tossed him over and over as it slid downhill. It filled his mouth with ice and snow each time he tried to breathe. As the avalanche slowed from 50 miles per hour (80.47 kilometers per hour) to 30 miles per hour (48.28 kilometers per hour), he began to sink. He said it was like "drowning to death, high in the mountains, in the middle of winter and miles from the nearest water."

When you have new snow and light winds it makes soft snow.

There are two kinds of slab avalanches. Some are soft and some are hard. Soft slab avalanches have soft snow. Soft slabs are also called storm slabs. This is because they form during a storm. This new slab of snow breaks up as it falls downhill. As it slides down the mountain, it turns into powdery chunks of snow.

Hard slab avalanches have hard snow. Snow gets harder in two different ways. Some hard slabs have old snow. Snow gets harder as it gets older.

Hard slabs can also be formed by strong winds. Hard slabs are stiff and thick. They stay together as they slide down the hillside. This makes them very dangerous.

Hard slabs are more difficult to trigger than soft slabs, but make a much larger and more deadly avalanche.

Did You Know?
According to the National Avalanche Center, soft slabs and hard slabs break in different ways. Soft slabs usually break under your feet. Hard slabs usually break after you move onto the slab.

crown

fracture line

flank

stauchwall

A slab has four sides. The top is called the **crown**. This is where the slab breaks. The line where it breaks is called the **fracture** line. This line is not always straight.

The sides of the slab are called **flanks**. There is one on the left and one on the right. Just like the crown, the flanks may not be straight.

The bottom of the slab is called the **stauchwall**. It is often destroyed during the slide down.

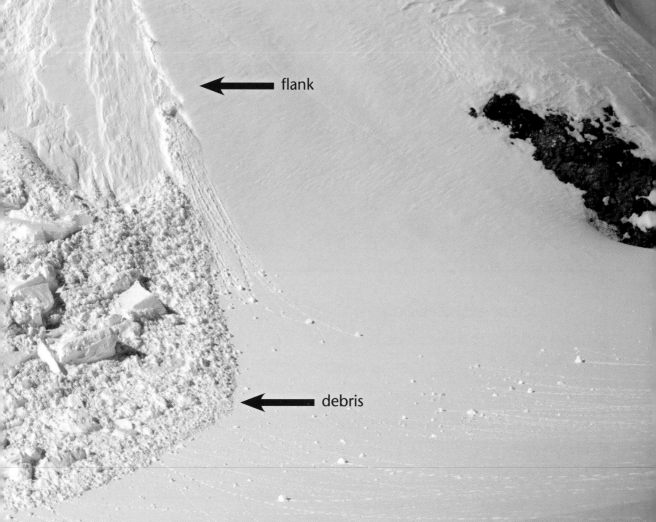

flank

debris

After the slab falls down, two more things appear. The bed under the slab is now visible. This is the slippery sliding surface that was underneath the slab.

At the bottom of the avalanche is a field of **debris**, or wreckage. The slab is all broken up. So is everything else that it pulled down the mountain.

In a slab avalanche, a slab of snow slides down the hill. The slab is one part of the avalanche. The slab is the top layer.

After the slab slides downhill, the bottom layer is very easy to see. The bottom layer of a slab avalanche is the sliding surface.

The third part of an avalanche is a weak layer of snow. This snow is between the slab and the sliding surface. Most avalanches occur when a weak layer fails.

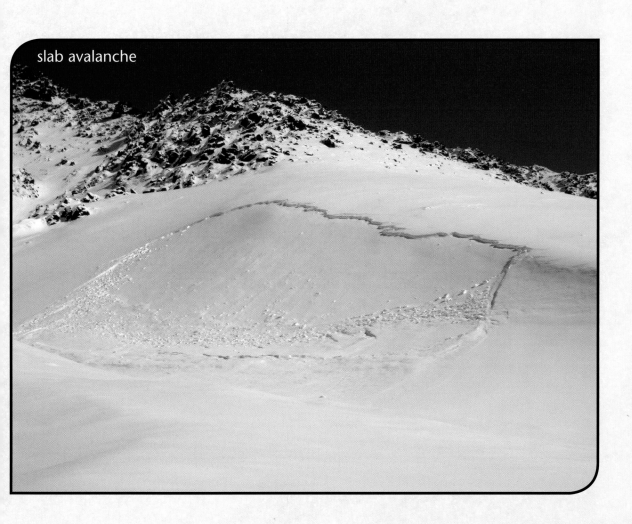

slab avalanche

What can form a weak layer? Put your glove into the snow and see. The first kind of weak layer can be seen on the top. The frost that develops on top of the snow is called surface hoar. Surface hoar is thin and weak. It forms when the air is wet and the wind is calm.

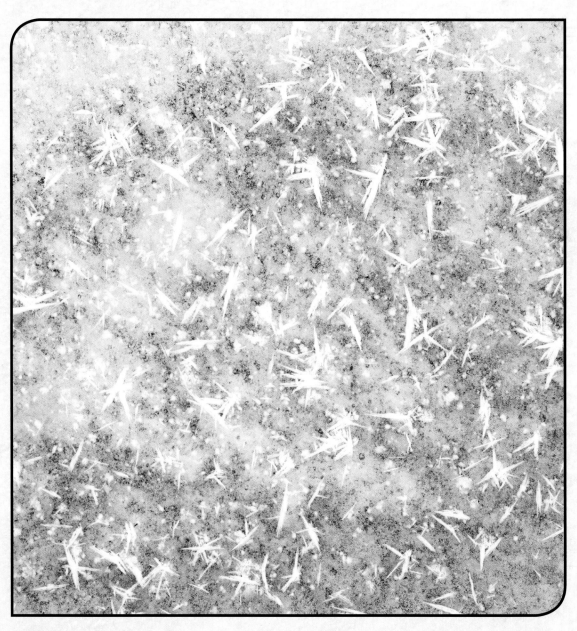

Surface hoar crystals are flat. Up close, the surface hoar crystals look like ferns.

Frost can also develop near the ground under the snow. This second kind of weak layer is called depth hoar or sugar snow. This type of weak layer is caused by a difference in temperatures. It forms when the ground is much warmer than the snow above it. This type of frost has crystals shaped like cups. You may see it when you dig your snow pit.

A difference in temperature also causes the third type of weak layer. Faceted snow crystals can develop near the surface of the snow. A facet is a flat, polished surface. Like gems with facets, this snow has sharp edges.

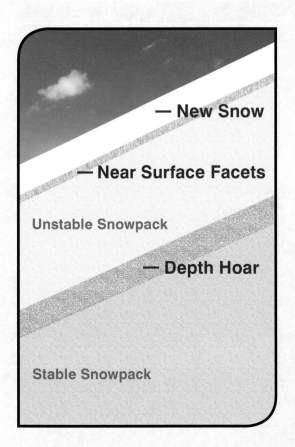

— New Snow

— Near Surface Facets

Unstable Snowpack

— Depth Hoar

Stable Snowpack

Depth hoar is found at the base of an Arctic snowpack.

The sliding surface in a slab avalanche is like a playground slide.

The bottom layer of a slab avalanche is the sliding surface. This layer is hard or slick and it slopes downhill. A sliding layer forms when a **crust** develops. There are three types and they all begin when water turns to ice.

The first type of crust can happen right before your eyes. When warm rain falls onto cold snow, it forms an ice crust.

The second type of crust forms when the rain and the snow are both a little warm. The rain seeps down into the snow and when it gets cold again, a rain crust forms.

The third crust that forms is a melt-freeze crust. The name of this crust describes how it forms. Warm weather melts the snow during the day and cold temperatures at night make it freeze again. The result is a slippery sliding surface.

Experienced backcountry travelers know how to find and test unstable snow layers.

Unstable Snowpack

The layers in a snowpack build up slowly over time. Some layers may be strong. Some layers may be weak. Will those layers cause an avalanche? If there is a slab on a weak layer on top of a sliding surface, the answer is yes!

New snow falls on top of old snow. Will the layers stick together? Or will the new layer slide off? That depends on the type of snow and the temperature. Cold snow crystals, such as stellars and dendrites, may not stick to old snow. Layers of old snow and new snow stick together better when the weather is warmer.

Stellar snowflakes have six wide arms.

Stellar dendrite snowflakes have branches like a tree.

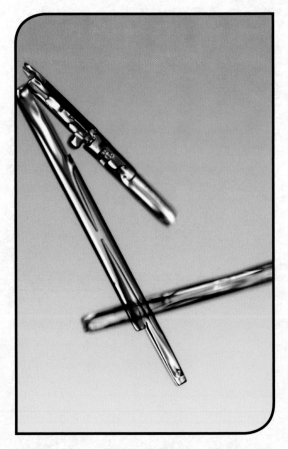

Needle snowflakes fall in warmer temperatures.

Ski Patrol

The Sun has just come up, and the ski patrol is hard at work. Members of the ski patrol dig snow pits to test for possible avalanches. They also use explosives for avalanche control. When the charge explodes, unstable snow slides down the mountain before anyone skis on it. The rest of the day, members of the ski patrol are on call to help with rescues.

Ski patrol teams use explosives to bring down loose snow before skiers use the slopes.

Rescue!

Can you rescue yourself? Can you save your own life? Do you know what to do when an avalanche starts? Experts say the best thing to do is to get out of the way. Move sideways and try to get off the slab. Let go of everything else. Hop off your snowmobile or your snowboard. Drop your poles and your skis. Try to hang onto the downside of a tree.

Did You Know?
According to the American Avalanche Association, 25 to 30 percent of the people caught in an avalanche die from their injuries. Someone buried in the snow has only a 30 percent chance of survival.

If the snow sweeps you away, keep your head up and your feet down. You want to go downhill on your back. Swim as hard as you can to get back up to the surface. Make an airspace for your mouth so you can breathe.

Panjshir ■
Afghanistan

Pakistan

India

Avalanches don't just affect skiers and backpackers. They also can have devastating effects on people who live in mountainous regions. A week of heavy snowstorms in Afghanistan triggered about 50 avalanches in Panjshir, Afghanistan, in March 2015. The slides killed about 200 people and injured dozens of others.

If you see someone buried by an avalanche, it is up to you to save them. You only have 15 minutes to find that person alive.

Go where you saw the person last. Ask the others on the slope to help you. Decide who will be the leader. Work together to make a plan.

Use the probe where the beacon shows the smallest number.

probe

avalanche shovel

Turn your rescue beacon to *receive* and listen closely. Can you hear the other person's beacon? Hold your beacon in front of you and follow the arrows. Each time the beacon makes a sound, move closer. When it reaches the lowest number, you are ready to use the **probe**. The small opening the probe makes will let in the air the victim needs. Then you can start digging.

beacon

Students practice rescue techniques before going into the backcountry.

If the victim does not have a beacon, check all of the places nearby that a person could get caught. Look for clues on the snow. Do you see the person's equipment? Lift each item one by one and listen for sound.

If you still don't see the missing person, you need to form a probe line. Everyone on the mountain should have a probe in their backpack. Make a long line and start probing. Move forward together in a grid search.

Always wear a beacon when you go into backcountry areas. It will make you easier to find!

This avalanche rescue dog can smell things buried deep in the snow.

Professional search and rescue crews work in the mountains. Some of these crews work with dogs. These avalanche rescue dogs travel with the crew wherever help is needed. They ride on ski lifts and travel on snowmobiles. They fly in helicopters and repel down. Just like the humans they work with, avalanche rescue dogs save lives.

Travel Safety

It's up to you to travel safely. Before you get out onto the slope, the avalanche forecasters have done their job. They checked the conditions in the local area. They issued their daily avalanche forecast. Did you check it before you went out?

Avalanche forecasters use a loupe and a crystal card to check the snow.

After you check the avalanche report, check the local conditions. Is it snowing or raining now? Was there a storm yesterday? New rain or snow changes the snowpack.

How steep are those slopes? Most avalanches happen on slopes that are 30 to 45 degrees. Use a tool called an inclinometer to check the incline. You can download it as an app for your smartphone.

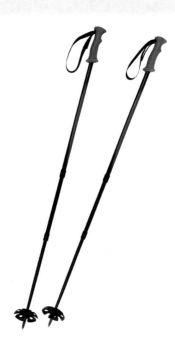

Some ski poles have a tool in the handle that measures the incline of a slope.

Did You Know?

Wind blows snow over the top of the hill. Sometimes the snow freezes there in a peak that looks like a wave. But this **cornice** will only hang in the air for a little while before it falls and causes an avalanche. Don't stand on it!

The wind is the next item to check. Look up and check for cornices at the top. These frozen waves will tell you which direction the wind is blowing.

Look at the slope farther down. Has the wind been blowing here too? Do you see any eroded snow? The wind has blown the smooth snow away. It has deposited the smooth snow in another place. These smooth pillows of snow form wind slabs.

After you've considered all these things, you can decide if it's a good day to head into the backcountry.

Eroded snow

Deposited snow

Eroded snow looks scratched up.
Deposited snow looks smooth and puffy.

Wind Watch
Strong wind can form a wind slab in minutes. If you hear a hollow drum sound when you walk on a snow pillow, get off immediately. You may trigger a slab avalanche!

How You Can Help When Disaster Strikes

Before you go out into the backcountry:
- Check the daily avalanche forecast
- Download avalanche apps to your phone
- Wear a rescue beacon
- Pack a first aid kit
- Bring an avalanche probe and shovel

On the slopes:
- Check the slope angle with an inclinometer
- Watch the wind
- Listen for nature's warning sounds

After an avalanche:
- Look before you move
- Ask others around you for help
- Work as a team
- Use your avalanche school training to help others in need

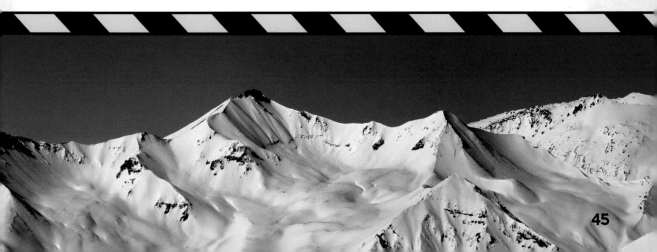

Glossary

avalanche (AV-uh-lanch): a large mass of snow sliding down a mountain

cornice (KAWR-nis): a mass of snow projecting over a mountain ridge

crown (kroun): the top of the slab

crust (kruhst): a hard external covering or coating

debris (duh-BREE): the remains at the bottom of the avalanche

flanks (flangks): the sides of something

fracture (FRAK-cher): to break or crack

powder (POU-der): loose, usually fresh snow

probe (prohb): a slender pole for exploring the depth of something

runout zone (RUHN-out zohn): the track where the avalanche ends

snowpack (SNOH-pak): the accumulation of winter snowfall, especially in mountain regions

stauchwall (STAK-vall): bottom wall, the bottom of the slab

Index

Show What You Know

1. What percentage of avalanche victims die in slides triggered by themselves or a member of their group?
2. Name the six red flags that let you know an avalanche is possible.
3. How does a weak layer form?
4. What are the most common slope inclines for avalanches?
5. Why is it so important to wear a beacon when you travel in the backcountry?

Websites to Visit

www.avalanche.org

www.fsavalanche.org

http://nsidc.org/cryosphere/snow/science/avalanches.html

About the Author

Anastasia Suen saw snow for the first time in the Sierra Nevada Mountains. She has also visited the Cascades and the Rockies. She lives with her family in Plano, Texas.

Meet The Author!
www.meetREMauthors.com

© 2016 Rourke Educational Media

www.rourkeeducationalmedia.com

PHOTO CREDITS: Cover © RaflaBelzowski; Title Page © KADimages; page 4 © diephosi; page 5 © Nina B; page 6 © yorkfoto; page 7 © Lopris; page 8 © mcseem; page 9 © Volt Collection; page 10 © ProPhotos; page 11 © Steve Heap; page 12 © fbxx, Marccophoto; page 13 © Image Source; page 14 © Pieter De Pauw; page 15 © ziggymaj, frontpoint; page 16 © NOAA; page 17 © bjdesign, karamysh; page 18 © technotr; page 19 © erectus; page 20 © tostphoto, Brenda Carson; page 21 © creativaimage; page 22 © Olivier Maire/epa/ Corbis; page 23 © wasja; page 24 © med_ved; page 25 © sandsun; page 26 © nicolamargaret; page 28 © ZargonDesign; page 30 © Vladimirovic; page 31 © frankljunior; page 32 © onfilm; page 33 © Clayoquot/Wikipedia; page 34 © Kichigin, Kenneth Libbrecht/Science Source; page 35 © Brett Pelletier; page 36 © Cyclonphoto; page 37 © Minko Chernev, jpa1999; page 38 © Komelau; page 39 © Minko Chernev; page 40 © PÃ©ter Gudella; page 41 © CyclonPhoto; page 42 © U.S. Geological Survey/Erich Peitzch; page 43 © trekandshoot, VichoT; page 44 © Duilio Fiorille, fbxx; page 45 © Anna Poltoraskaya

Edited by: Keli Sipperley
Cover and interior design by: Jen Thomas

Library of Congress PCN Data

Avalanches / Anastasia Suen
(Devastating Disasters)
ISBN 978-1-63430-424-5 (hard cover)
ISBN 978-1-63430-524-2 (soft cover)
ISBN 978-1-63430-614-0 (e-Book)
Library of Congress Control Number: 2015931737

Printed in the United States of America, North Mankato, Minnesota

Also Available as:
ROURKE'S
e-Books